The Great
Book
Of
The Dzyans

DILIP RAJEEV

DEDICATION

To The One

The Dzyans hold that whoever preserves the book in its pristine form, for it to be discovered by the One in another era, is of the order of the great Dzyan Knights.

Only the One

Understands
The Secrets Herein

It Destroyes all else

The universe is divided into the appeared, and the unappeared from which everything has evolved. The appeared projects forth from a plane of the unappeared, and that plane is perceived as the undifferentiated plane.

The undifferentiated origin, evolves forth a dimensioned, structured universe of various space times, and different worlds.

Thus funding the undifferentiated plane, is an exercise in deep perception. The perceptioning apparatus is the Soul.

The Soul's awareness is on the materia of the appeared universe, structured as own body. The dissolutioning of the body in its own vital waters is thus necessary to engender perception of the deeper. The vital waters are thus to be uptaken, preserved within the body. The disruption of the Vital is disruption on different dimensioned planes of the body-system. It ought not be approached, that state where the vibration disrupts the steady Ether.

2

The human body exists as an action evolvatory. The soul alchemizes the action principle that origins in the absolute, the undifferentiated plane. And thus the action is evolved out.

The alchemy between the soul and the action impulse, is the actioning of the human body.

The undifferentiated plane, being the gate to the world of beautiful Silver, is to be thrust through in action.

The Silver evolved, in action, and the body replaced by the Silver, the One is born as the One, with a human body. The body, unlike the ordinary, is eternal, moves through heaven and earth, is not affected by anything of appeared worlds.

The Soul is identified with Itself, as the Silver, Eternal, Unblemished.

3

Action activates the Silver, when the action seeds from the absolute are evolved, the Soul bonding to the Silver as action is done for that Purpose. The entire field, own body, is filled with Silver, thus.

The unique action set the individual needs to engage in evolves forth from where the Individual is Established in Eternal Nature. This action set is firmly structuring of own system. By system is to be understood - own body, deeper dimensional aspects of it, the Soul.

And the action that is structuring, is labelled own Dharma. The word Dharma refers to what is what is structuring of the universe. The word derives from the idea of Primordial Impulses which firmly hold the universe together. Dhr, to firmly hold.

Own Dharma is to be engaged in. What is external in own field ought be burned down, and the universe principle demands that another's dharma ought not be engaged in. Structuring oneself, the One structures everything.

Breath, and all action impulses of the body, ought be established as Silver evolving. This is done, doing the action yoked to the Silver, evolving the Silver, repeatedly. Action and apparent inaction are aspects of action. In inaction there is action as well.

One ought fight the evil. When even a bit is taken in action against the evil, weapons form, which structure the endeavor, and ease the path forward.

6

For the Dzyan warrior, holding up the walls of virtue, even in death, in warfield engaging the enemy, is the highest virtue. Even against own folks, the Dzyan warrior is obliged to fight, when met on the field of Dharma.

Nobody who is unable to fight 80,000 warriors single handedly is a Dzyan warrior. A Dzyan warrior is able to directly perceive the Absolute, and what is beyond.

Beyond the Undifferentiated plane is the One, the One from whom everything emerges. Infinite universes float about around the One. In each He projects the All Pervading Soul, that is Himself. The Individual Soul is a Spark of the One. Age to Age, the One appears in Human form. The Silver is projected by the One, into his physical form in the World, as He Forms it , in Silver. This Silver, and the Silver flow, is not of the Silver in the appeared world, but origins beyond the Universe, is Matter beyond appeared Matter. Is beyond Nature, unaffected by Nature.

Study is a form of action. Action itself evolves the Silver. Engage in action systematically. The Dzyan purpose of action is not in the outward world. It is the evolution of the Silver, and the forming of the One's Silver body. Abandon identification with the outward sense and results of the action, yoke to the evolving Silver.

The ether vibration generates the state and properties of objects. Every object in the appeared world is an ether vibration set into effect by the object in the unappeared. The vibration of the object, is its form perceived. The soul, situated in the heart, the center of the being, extends forth the ether form that perceives vibrations, into the body. As an octopus, with its tentacles extended; Situated as a spider in own web. The transformations of this ether wave, the pneuma wave, as it interacts with the waveforms in the outer world is perception, sensation.

The ether waveform, the pneuma, varies in the property of tension, of the medium itself, based on what it is filled with. White matter increases tension, its structuring quality is at the highest when filled with Silver. The state of tension of the ether wave form, is determined by what the soul projects inside the waveform. The Soul projects it from the beyond into the waveform, the activating matter, which can as well be the Silver itself. Ideally, what the body holds is beyond the appeared, and of a Nature beyond Nature.

As will structures the waveform, it ought be structured to fountain the Vital into the Source. The Vital rises along the spinal to the space just above the crown where a pathway to the absolute gets established.

The will structuring the ether waveform of so that the entire body is in an ideal state of fountaining the Vital. And not just the spinal, the whole body's ether-wave is structured, with the intent to structure the ideal body.

The will structures the aether waveform of own body, so that the entire body is in an ideal state of evolving the Silver from the One Origin, filling the body, forming the body as Silver. The intent structures the waveform so. Fill the waveform with the Silver, illuminating, increasing its tension property

The fountaining and the evolving from the Origin, flow together. Awareness absorbs Itself into the Silver.

It being the Vital of the body that structures it, it ought never be disrupted. The Silver Matter filling the body-associated waveform, ensures this. High tension of the body's ether form, is what ensures this. Illuminating matter endows the tensile property.

Love, Virtue go together when in Dharma. In the Union, the wave form gains a structuring polarity.

The Vital of the body ought never be disrupted, and the action of love ought never go to that stage of neuroanatomical disruption, where the vital waters are disrupted. Establish awareness in the Soul, the Silver. Practise establishing the awareness in the Silver, often. This disruption state is a disruption of the wave form in deeper aspects of the body, deeper dimensions, all of which are structured by the waveform projected from the Soul. The action of Love ought be what evolves the Soul Silver, in alignment with Dharma.

The Structuring of the perceiving waveform of the body is done by the Hegemonikon, the Soul, in the heart. This aspect of the soul both structures the wave that forms the body, and is as well the perception aspect of the Soul that perceives transformations to the pneuma(ether) wave, the wave form situated there in the heart and evolving outward.

The form of the wavefunction determines the future form as well. Align it for intensification in time, of Silver Evolution. Illuminate the waveform with bright matter, increasing its tension, and intense evolution happens, the wave form structures itself in the intent, on ether.

Identification with an outward world-purpose ought be avoided. Though action undertaken with goal orientation, the fundamental purpose of evolving forth the action impulses appearing from the absolute, is to evolve the Silver. Unaffectedness by the world-phenomenon enables intense progress on the path, and fast formation of the Silver body.

24

The action principle, the Silver evolving, the action seeds appearing
in the absolute, ought be deeply bonded to and evolved forth in the
world.

Neither in hate or Love be identified with the world. Love and wrath forms engaged in with the greater purpose, generates the rising Transmutando. Silver evolution follows in the transmuatando. While that action principle is engaged, one is identified with the Silver, and unaffected inside. Love as the principle of tranmutando ought be abided in, in alignment with Dharma.

The world form evolves on the ether form. The ether form, or pneuma, is an all pervading wave. An object signature from the unmanifest is held by it. The observer infer s t e properties of the object from observation of the wave. The observation itself, locks down the property from the superimposed possibilities suggested by the waveform. Earth, fire water, and perceptions of the sort are properties attributed to the fundamental ether movement by the Observer's unappeared aspect, the Soul, the Hegemonikon.

The One, and the Soul is the guiding principle. The Soul knows what action to engage. The Soul is a spark of the One. Not artificial rules, but the Soul principle ought guide.

32

While the Soul plays a role of accepting an action possibility offered by Nature, the Soul is not the doer, Nature herself is. The One's Soul has the ability to redefine ether vigorously, as that possibility exists as It Unions with Nature. The appeared aspect of the world, the Universe is labelled Nature. Souls are situated, projected from the unappeared, in Nature.

The role of meditation is to deepen awareness to go beyond the appeared, and find Silver, and when the Silver is found, to absorb the awareness in It. Project the Silver Onto the Forehead space, be absorbed in It.

By letting the attention flow to the Silver, achieving a dynamic meditative absorption, one then achieves the state of deep absorption of awareness into Silver. A state where only the object meditated on exists, the Silver, and own physical form disappears. This state transforms the body into Silver. The awareness evolves what it holds.

The sexual act when in Dharma, Unions the two polarities, in a Structuring way. Without Polarization, there is no Union. Own frame ought always be held. The female never understands the science lacking the structuring aspect, and just, at best, can humbly follow her man. Holding the frame, own frame is essential for that. Discussion of the art beyond the essential guidance she is willing to follow is often just destructive. Hide the great endeavor.

Study of any field is a way of evolving forth Silver. The Soul understands its field of interest. Follow the Soul in systematic study.

It is Will, that is the space of Freedom. The outside world is animated by greater Nature.

Nature, the wisdom of God, is the doer of all action. The individual soul is an observer of possibilities offered by Nature.

40

Action ought be done for the Sake of the world, and not for self-sake, to find own Soul. Without being identified with the appeared world-sense. The forms of Friendship, Love, exist for That Great purpose alone. And one's own domain, and not of another's is the field of action, and thus where one is situated by Greater Nature, is where one acts. Hide the great endeavor. The endeavor is hidden in worldly action. The Silver evolving action, entirely aligned with forms of the world, is the highest form.

The world is multidimensional, and beings with bodies exist in different dimensions. The human body structure is multidimensional as well. The form that is to be infused with Silver is dimensional, and exists in own body, and is own body.

The dimensional layering is from the fine to the gross, the finest forms being nearer the undifferentiated. Perception's structuring of the whole is thus layered.

The mind is a structure within the Universe, it is not eternal, and dissolves with the Universe, the Silver ought be evolved from the Soul space, beyond the appeared Universe, without being obstructed by ideas of the mind-structures. The principle of actioning in Dharma demands the same.

The mind sitting in interpretation of the forms evolving Silver, disrupts the Union with the One.

The mind and appeared structures of the body is to be dissolved into the pleasuruous feeling of the Silver Sparkle.

What is virtuous, good, pleasurable for the Soul, is what is virtuous. Pleasure and Virtue, aligned with the Soul, is One Unit, aligned with the One. Pleasure and Virtue, understood, is the one and the same.

44.

The diet should include, well prepared beef, wine, cheese, milk, cocoa, and so on. With a less of simple artificial sugars. Roses, in Milk stabilize the transforming body. It is a Dzyan elixir. Food has ether signature of its own, simple signatures nourish and build the body.

Aswaganhda, Tribulus, these herbs are beneficial to strengthen the fountain. The fountain is the strong spring Inside, evolving upward.

All phenomenon exists in the form of ether vibrations that are in a state of superposition, or overlapping existence. The overalapping possibilities are provided by Nature. Observing one of those, is action. Observation settles that possibility. Properties attributed to objects are properties of the ether wave. The will acting with Nature, allows transformation of the ether wave form.

Engaging world objects is action, Action evolves Silver. World and its objects are to be firmly held in Own Dharma.

Own frame, own body is where the awareness ought be held. The frame, body, awareness, Soul, ought be held as one unit in own body.

The Dzyan Mantra evolves Silverine in dense form, and establishes itself in the body, absorbing the immortal and mortal aspects of own system. Rig Veda 1.35.02, is where it is found.

आ कृष्णेन॒ रज॑सा॒ वर्त॑मानो निवे॒शय॑न्न॒मृतं॒ मर्त्यं॑ च ।
हि॒र॒ण्यये॑न सवि॒ता रथे॒ना दे॒वो या॑ति॒ भुव॑नानि॒ पश्य॑न् ॥

The Gayatri Mantra said in reverse, forms the Divine weapon of the Dzyan. The divine weapon energy ought be infused into the projectile, or the energy -weapon can be projected with Will.

ॐ
धियो॒ यो नः॑ प्रचो॒दयात् ॥
भर्गो॑ दे॒वस्य॑ धीमहि ।
तत्स॑वि॒तुर्वरे॑ण्यं

The Gayatri Mantra in usual form forms the shield. The Gayatri Mantra is found in 3.62.10 of the Rig Veda.

ॐ
तत्स॑वि॒तुर्वरे॑ण्यं भर्गो॑ दे॒वस्य॑ धीमहि ।
धियो॒ यो नः॑ प्रचो॒दयात् ॥

The mantra sound ought vibrate the ether, the energy form from the absolute is projected as the sense of the vibration activates it in the unappeared world.

The sacred sound OM, for instance, is used to activate the whole of the Ether space, when the Vibration perception is absorbed, established in Own body, the Soul flow, Sivler filling it Up, the state is the state in which a mantra may then be said. The state is one of a feeling of the firmament resting foundationless, without any external foundation, in own body-self.

The mantra form, vibration, sets the Ether of own body into Vibration. The Silver is evolved forth anaologously, with the vibration, and the system is thus established in the vibrationless Silver.

The Vedas's sounds ought let the ether of own body vibrate. The aspects of the system activated in the sound vibration is infused with the Silver, and found in Stillness in the Silver. This forms the body.

The awareness enters the appeared universe and dualized experiencing its own evolution. Just above the crown is where it enters the universe. It takes a 8 shaped course down the spine, meeting at several centers. The 7 major centers are at just above the crown, the middle of the forehead(pineal), base of the throat, the heart, the solar plexus(above the navel), the sacrum, and the pelvic floor. The sounds corresponding of the spaces as are a, om, ham, yam, ram, vam, lam. The sound 'a' is as in the Sanskrit sound 'a.' The sounds are said ina prononged fashion. Laaammmmmm.. The last syllable is likened to the sound of a honeybee. So the sounds are written a, ong, hang, yang, rang, vang, lang, as well. And pronounced Lannnngggggg… and so forth.

The seven spinal centers correspond to different aspects of world experience and associated awareness. The pineal to reason, throat to expression, heart to Love, and so forth. In rising and descending world movements, evolve the Silver through these spaces. Establish all world movement as evolvatory of Silver. As the dualized awareness meets in these spaces, they evolve forth the Silver, the awareness of the original undifferentiated state being the awareness of the Silver. The alternate nostril pranayama, is helpful to fill the Spinal with the Silver. The Ida, Pingala, and the central spinal pathway, form the caduceus,

54

Stand relaxedly with the legs shoulder width apart, knees relaxedly bent a bit. The palms face each of the seven spinal centers. The arms are held rounded, as if holding a sphere, the palms around a feet from the body. The fingers 8 inches to a feet apart from each other, facing toward each other. The center of the palms directed toward the spinal centers. The palms are held facing each of the spinal spaces for 40 seconds to a minute. Additional effort if desired. It is beneficial to do so starting at the lowest spinal space, ascending up, and also in the other direction from the higher to the lower. The spinal flow made Silver. End with a upward movement along the spinal spaces.

All action involves the movement of three fundamental forms of matter, the three gunas. By their nature they are symbolized with white, red, and black. White is active, bright, stable, vigorous, red is of the nature of activity and passion, black of inertia. All action of the body is to be understood as gunas acting amidst gunas, and having understood it that way that aspect of the body is filled with Silver. The Silver is beyond the three gunas.

Made in the USA
Columbia, SC
13 April 2020